HIP-HOP

Alicia Keys
Ashanti
Beyoncé
Black Eyed Peas
Busta Rhymes
Chris Brown
Christina Aguilera
Ciara
Cypress Hill
Daddy Yankee
DMX
Don Omar
Dr. Dre
Eminem
Fat Joe
50 Cent
The Game
Hip-Hop: A Short History
Hip-Hop Around the World
Ice Cube
Ivy Queen
Jay-Z
Jennifer Lopez
Juelz Santana
Kanye West

Lloyd Banks
Ludacris
Mariah Carey
Mary J. Blige
Missy Elliot
Nas
Nelly
Notorious B.I.G.
OutKast
Pharrell Williams
Pitbull
Queen Latifah
Reverend Run (of Run DMC)
Sean "Diddy" Combs
Snoop Dogg
T.I.
Tupac
Usher
Will Smith
Wu-Tang Clan
Xzibit
Young Jeezy
Yung Joc

It might be hard to picture gangsta rapper Ice Cube as the star of family-friendly films, but he is. This megastar has many sides.

Hip-Hop

Ice Cube

Toby G. Hamilton

Mason Crest Publishers

Produced by Harding House Publishing Service, Inc.
201 Harding Avenue, Vestal, NY 13850.

MASON CREST PUBLISHERS INC.
370 Reed Road
Broomall, Pennsylvania 19008
(866)MCP-BOOK (toll free)
www.masoncrest.com

Printed in the United States of America

First Printing

9 8 7 6 5 4 3 2 1

Library of Congress Cataloging-in-Publication Data

Hamilton, Toby G.
  Ice Cube / Toby G. Hamilton.
     p. cm. — (Hip-hop)
  Includes bibliographical references and index.
  ISBN 978-1-4222-0294-4
  ISBN: 978-1-4222-0077-3 (series)
  1. Ice Cube (Musician)—Juvenile literature. 2. Rap musicians—United States—Biography—Juvenile literature. 3. Actors—United States—Biography—Juvenile literature. I. Title.
ML3930.I34H36 2008
782.421649092—dc22
[B]
                              2007030442

Publisher's notes:
• All quotations in this book come from original sources and contain the spelling and grammatical inconsistencies of the original text.

• The Web sites mentioned in this book were active at the time of publication. The publisher is not responsible for Web sites that have changed their addresses or discontinued operation since the date of publication. The publisher will review and update the Web site addresses each time the book is reprinted.

DISCLAIMER: The following story has been thoroughly researched, and to the best of our knowledge, represents a true story. While every possible effort has been made to ensure accuracy, the publisher will not assume liability for damages caused by inaccuracies in the data, and makes no warranty on the accuracy of the information contained herein. This story has not been authorized nor endorsed by Ice Cube.

Contents

Hip-Hop Time Line

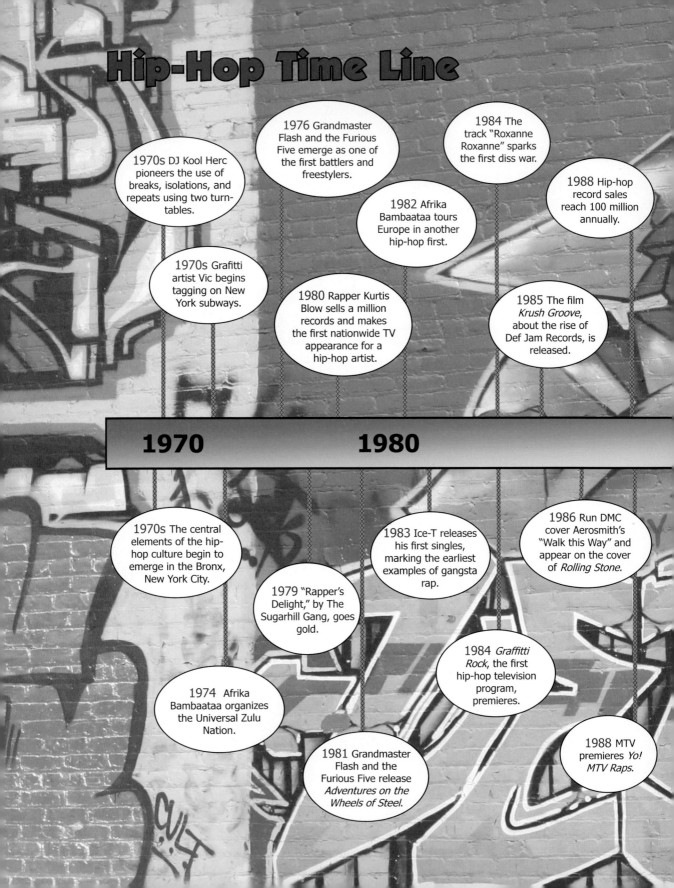

1976 Grandmaster Flash and the Furious Five emerge as one of the first battlers and freestylers.

1984 The track "Roxanne Roxanne" sparks the first diss war.

1970s DJ Kool Herc pioneers the use of breaks, isolations, and repeats using two turntables.

1988 Hip-hop record sales reach 100 million annually.

1982 Afrika Bambaataa tours Europe in another hip-hop first.

1970s Grafitti artist Vic begins tagging on New York subways.

1980 Rapper Kurtis Blow sells a million records and makes the first nationwide TV appearance for a hip-hop artist.

1985 The film *Krush Groove*, about the rise of Def Jam Records, is released.

1970

1980

1970s The central elements of the hip-hop culture begin to emerge in the Bronx, New York City.

1983 Ice-T releases his first singles, marking the earliest examples of gangsta rap.

1986 Run DMC cover Aerosmith's "Walk this Way" and appear on the cover of *Rolling Stone*.

1979 "Rapper's Delight," by The Sugarhill Gang, goes gold.

1974 Afrika Bambaataa organizes the Universal Zulu Nation.

1984 *Graffitti Rock*, the first hip-hop television program, premieres.

1981 Grandmaster Flash and the Furious Five release *Adventures on the Wheels of Steel*.

1988 MTV premieres *Yo! MTV Raps*.

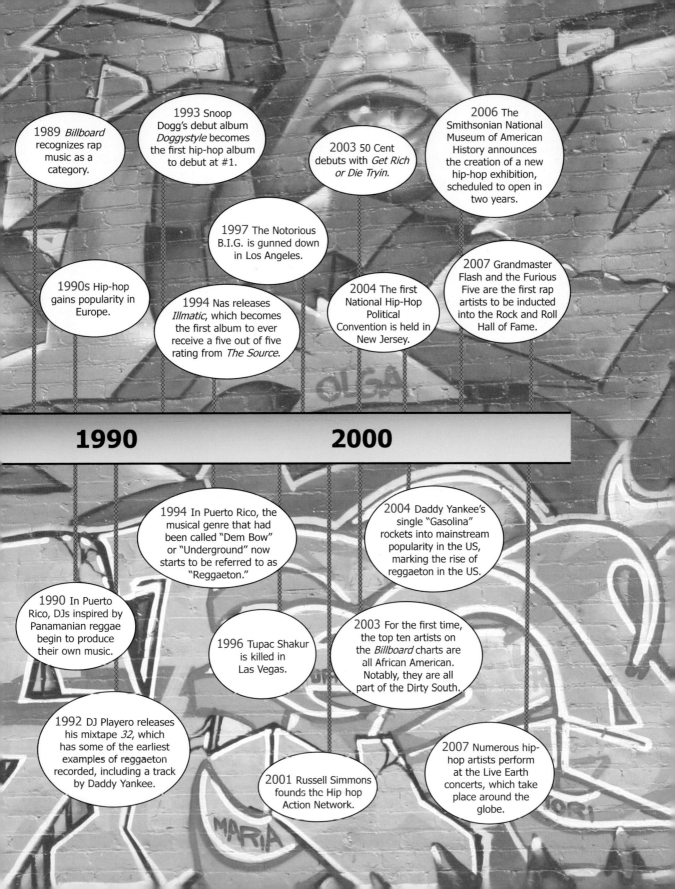

1989 *Billboard* recognizes rap music as a category.

1993 Snoop Dogg's debut album *Doggystyle* becomes the first hip-hop album to debut at #1.

2003 50 Cent debuts with *Get Rich or Die Tryin.*

2006 The Smithsonian National Museum of American History announces the creation of a new hip-hop exhibition, scheduled to open in two years.

1997 The Notorious B.I.G. is gunned down in Los Angeles.

1990s Hip-hop gains popularity in Europe.

1994 Nas releases *Illmatic*, which becomes the first album to ever receive a five out of five rating from *The Source*.

2004 The first National Hip-Hop Political Convention is held in New Jersey.

2007 Grandmaster Flash and the Furious Five are the first rap artists to be inducted into the Rock and Roll Hall of Fame.

1990

2000

1994 In Puerto Rico, the musical genre that had been called "Dem Bow" or "Underground" now starts to be referred to as "Reggaeton."

2004 Daddy Yankee's single "Gasolina" rockets into mainstream popularity in the US, marking the rise of reggaeton in the US.

1990 In Puerto Rico, DJs inspired by Panamanian reggae begin to produce their own music.

1996 Tupac Shakur is killed in Las Vegas.

2003 For the first time, the top ten artists on the *Billboard* charts are all African American. Notably, they are all part of the Dirty South.

1992 DJ Playero releases his mixtape *32*, which has some of the earliest examples of reggaeton recorded, including a track by Daddy Yankee.

2001 Russell Simmons founds the Hip hop Action Network.

2007 Numerous hip-hop artists perform at the Live Earth concerts, which take place around the globe.

Ice Cube has the hip-hop attitude. He can spit out some of the most profane lyrics around—Sometimes it seems as though he invites controversy. Still, he knows when to turn off the venom.

Hip-Hop Attitude

If you've seen Ice Cube in recent movies like *Are We There Yet?* and *Are We Done Yet?* he might seem like just another comic actor in a family-friendly movie. You might not guess that when Ice Cube's career began, he was one of the most controversial and feared of a new breed of musical artists: gangsta rappers. Today Ice Cube is popular with all kinds of audiences, but in his early days he was one of the most hardcore rappers around. He pioneered gangsta rap by spitting **venomous** lyrics filled with profanity, violence, **sexism**, and other hate-filled messages. When he started in the music business, he was just a teenager. In those angry youthful days, he made a name for himself with lyrics about dealing dope and killing cops. No one listening to the vicious young rapper would have guessed that one day Ice Cube would star on the big screen in family-friendly comedies.

From New York to L.A.

Ice Cube's professional rap career began in the late 1980s in California. The young rapper grew up in South Central Los Angeles's dangerous neighborhoods. It was a rough world filled with gangs, drugs, racism, and violence. By the late eighties, Ice Cube and other South Central hip-hop artists were ready to bring their inner-city reality to the world. They would do so with a new form of hardcore, hard-hitting music that would shock audiences all around the world.

At that time, the fastest growing music in America was hip-hop. Hip-hop began in the 1970s as party music, in the streets and clubs of some of New York City's toughest neighborhoods. DJs spinning dance music began cutting and mixing songs using two turntables. They also started "toasting," or calling out to the audience, over the music. Those two innovations, both of which had their roots in Jamaican music, evolved into a new type of music called hip-hop. The *sampling* and mixing of songs became an art form that DJs used to create beat-heavy, danceable tunes. Toasting also got more complex, until MCs were speaking in a style of rhythm and rhyme that would become known as rapping, and which gave hip-hop music its other name—rap.

Hip-hop music was born in the New York ghetto, but it spread like wildfire to other American cities. Long before hip-hop hit *mainstream* radio, inner-city kids were setting up turntables, spinning records, writing rhymes, and rapping with their friends. By the1980s, hip-hop had made its way to California and taken root in the tough neighborhoods of South Central Los Angeles. On those streets, hip-hop would be reborn. In New York's neighborhoods, hip-hop developed first as dance music. In L.A.'s dangerous hoods, hip-hop morphed into a new form: gangsta rap. Ice Cube would be one of its most important pioneers.

Music to Live By

Ice Cube was just a kid when he heard hip-hop music for the first time, but it changed his life. He was ten years old and sitting in the car on the way to something every kid dreads: the dentist. But other than the dreaded appointment with the dentist's chair, the day promised to be like any other . . . until

The earliest music was just a voice and a drum. Hip-hop connected to these earliest roots.

Hip-hop eventually made its way to the streets of California cities such as Los Angeles. But this hip-hop was different. It talked about guns, violence, and killing. It wasn't always about dancing and having fun.

his uncle slipped a tape into the stereo. The music hailed from the East Coast, from New York in fact. The group was the Sugarhill Gang. The song was "Rapper's Delight." It was the first rap single to break through to the pop airwaves and have widespread success. It hit the top-40 on the popular music charts in the United States and changed hip-hop music forever. When that young boy heard it in his uncle's car, it blew his mind. The dentist appointment was probably a rather easy affair that day, because all Ice Cube could think about was the song that had just rocked his world.

The thing that audiences found so intoxicating about "Rapper's Delight," and hip-hop music in general, was that it came from the street, from the real world. There were no symphonies, or complex melodies, or vocal acrobatics. The music was refreshingly simple: just a beat and a rap. There was something basic and instinctual about it, something pure and inviting and intimately expressive. Like the earliest forms of music, which consisted of just a drum and a voice, this was music of the people, by the people, and for the people. Anyone could be a part of hip-hop music; all you needed was a rhythm and a rhyme.

Hip-hop, however, wasn't just about music. It was a whole culture that was developing in the streets of urban America. Hip-hop was about people, mostly young people from underprivileged backgrounds, claiming the street, making a name for themselves, and earning respect from their peers. In New York City's black and Latino communities, where hip-hop began, young people had to deal with a lot of problems; poverty, racism, and crime were everyday realities in their neighborhoods. There weren't a lot of opportunities for success and respect in the ghetto, and young people searched for a way to express themselves and be part of something big.

Hip-Hop: An American Dream

By the 1970s, decades of racism and *segregationist* policies had left their mark on America's minority communities. The civil rights movement had done a lot to bring America's deeply embedded policies and attitudes of racism and discrimination out into the open, but it would take much longer to begin turning around the effects of nearly two-hundred years of discrimination. America was supposed to be the land of opportunity. According to the "American dream," everybody, no matter what their backgrounds, could pull themselves up by their bootstraps, work hard, and become a success.

The American dream no doubt proved true for many people, but not for everyone. Plenty of people worked hard in back-breaking jobs, but couldn't climb out of crushing poverty. A lot of those people were members of minority groups. In the 1970s, being black or Latino in America virtually guaranteed that there would be roadblocks on the path to success and respect. For too many minority kids in poverty-stricken urban America, one message seemed clear: the American dream was for the white and the already wealthy. If they wanted respect, recognition, and success, they'd have to find it another way.

Hip-hop became a new expression of the American dream in the country's toughest neighborhoods. Poverty, racism, and other disadvantages made trying to pull oneself up by one's bootstraps like trying to climb a greased pole out of the ghetto: a slippery business that, while possible for a few, left others lying on the ground dirty, humiliated, and exhausted. But hip-hop allowed people to pull themselves up with music, dance, and artistic expression. Young people in New York City, and later in other cities around America, found that hip-hop culture allowed them to stake a claim in their chaotic world, make a name for themselves, and earn some respect.

While the music would become the most famous element of hip-hop culture, it also contained other important elements.

One was a new form of street dancing called b-boying, or break dancing. Another was laying claim to public space by tagging it with a spray-painted name or symbol. The dancing and graffiti that developed alongside DJing and MCing were all part of hip-hop culture, and they were all a form of rebellion against a world that wanted to deny the existence of the minority communities in America's ghettos. The hip-hop culture they created would one day become so popular it would affect film, television, music, dance, art, fashion, and even language all over the world.

Playful, Political, and Powerful

At first, hip-hop music was all about the party. The beats were for dancing. The rhymes were for the crowd's entertainment. But hip-hop quickly developed a competitive edge. MCs made boasts and brags about their skills. Then they started dissing other MCs. Rapping soon became a way to do battle, with rappers fighting each other with their lyrics. Rivalries developed, some friendly, and some more serious. B-boys (and b-girls) also battled each other, getting down on the dance floor with body-bending, mind-blowing moves. Taggers and graffiti crews got into the competitive spirit as well, and graffiti exploded into (at its best) a colorful, complex public art form.

Rappers, however, didn't stay focused on themselves and their skills for long. The brags and boasts, of course, would always remain a defining element of rap music and just get bigger as the years went on, but rappers began to look outward as well. They commented on the world around them, penning insightful rhymes about the trappings of the ghetto and urban life. They talked about social problems like poverty, racism, and crime. A highly political form of hip-hop, called conscious hip-hop, developed. It not only commented on many social problems, it hoped to actually help change things by raising awareness about the problems experienced by people living in the inner city.

Hip-hop was born in New York City, all the way across the country from where Ice Cube grew up. Hip-hop was a way for urban young people to have fun—and to send a message to the outside world about what life was really like for them.

Hip-hop's musical evolution didn't stop there. As the music moved around the country, it continued to grow and change. Every rapper brought a different world experience and point of view to the craft. Regional artists and styles developed. Hip-hop developed radio popularity, but East Coast artists and styles dominated the budding industry. But as the music spread to the West Coast, things began to change. In South Central Los Angeles, the worst neighborhoods were seething with gang violence, mostly between the Crips and the Bloods. Those dangerous streets would prove to be a fertile breeding ground for the hardest-hitting form of rap of all. No one knew it at the time, but the day Ice Cube's uncle put "Rapper's Delight" on for his nephew to hear, the first seeds of gangsta rap were planted. In just a few years, Ice Cube would be one of the founding fathers of the hardest-hitting form of rap and the most controversial music **genre** in the world.

Though his neighborhood wasn't entirely safe, young Ice Cube had it better than many of the other kids living there. His parents were supportive, and he stayed away from gangs. It might seem odd, then, that he became one of the biggest names in gangsta rap.

Unlikely Prophet

If you look at his early life, Ice Cube actually seems an unlikely candidate to become one of gangsta rap's prophets. Although he was born and raised in the Crip-dominated Crenshaw neighborhood, he wasn't a gangbanger like many of his peers. He was luckier than a lot of young people he knew. He had caring parents who encouraged him in his sports, academics, and artistic pursuits. He also had an older brother, Clyde, who warned him to stay away from gangs, dealing, and the trappings of street life. All in all, his family did a good job of sheltering Ice Cube from South Central's front lines. But they couldn't shelter him completely. That life was all around him, touching everything, and eventually it would be the major influence on Ice Cube's music.

Born and Raised

Ice Cube was born O'Shea Jackson on June 15, 1969. He was the fourth child, and his parents, Hosea and Doris, wanted to give him a special name. In 1969, a star college football player from California was entering his rookie year in the

O'Shea Jackson—Ice Cube—was named for one of the biggest names in football. O. J. Simpson was a big success at the University of Southern California and went on to a hall-of-fame career as a member of the Buffalo Bills. He later gained infamy as an alleged double murderer.

NFL. His name was O. J. Simpson, and he was quickly becoming one of the most admired black men in America. After a record-smashing college football career, he looked like he had a bright future ahead of him, and Hosea and Doris chose his name for their newest child. They softened the "j" sound to a "sh" sound, and named their new son O'Shea. Since his last name was Jackson, his initials would also be O. J.

Hosea and Doris had good jobs, he as a machinist and she as a clerk. They provided a relatively comfortable life for their children. But still, the declining South Central neighborhoods were all around, and they worried that the streets would suck their kids in. But O'Shea's childhood was quite sheltered, at least in the early days. He loved sports and developed a bit of a reputation in the neighborhood as a jock. He was especially good at basketball and football. His speed on the football field earned further comparisons to O. J. Simpson, who was a running back. In the sports world, O. J. was called "The Juice." On the street, O'Shea's friends started calling him "Juice" as well.

Sports weren't young O'Shea's only interests. He was also quite artistic and enjoyed drawing. He wasn't bad at school either. He wasn't a straight-A student, but he kept up good grades, usually B's, and excelled at math. In those early years, O'Shea didn't have much connection to music. Like any other kid, he enjoyed listening to music, and when he heard "Rapper's Delight" at ten years old, it totally altered his perspective. But still, growing up he didn't play any musical instruments or sing, so he probably would have been surprised if you had told him he'd be a musical *icon* one day.

A Wake-Up Call

In interviews, Ice Cube always says that, as a child, it was his family who had the biggest influence on him. While his friends were idolizing actors, musicians, athletes, and other famous people, O'Shea admired the people most involved in his life. In a chat for the Rap News Network, he said that his father and brother were the people he looked up to most:

> *"I was fortunate to have my father and brother with me. My brother is nine years older than myself. I looked up to both of them because they were always available, always there with anything I needed to help me get through the day, you know, living in South Central Los Angeles and trying not to get caught in all the traps it had. So I have to say my father and my brother had the biggest influence on me."*

Perhaps the biggest trap South Central had was gangs. They made the streets a dangerous place. In many ways, it didn't matter whether you were in a gang or not, they could still affect you. You could still get beat up for wearing the wrong colors or jumped for living in the wrong neighborhood. You could still get struck by a stray bullet in a drive-by shooting. For some young people, those harsh realities don't faze them. One of the things about youth is the way it sometimes makes you feel as though nothing can hurt you and nothing bad is ever going to happen to you. But when O'Shea was just twelve years old, that illusion was broken. One day he found out just how dangerous life could be and how quickly everything could come to an end. In the Rap News Network chat, he described that day as a major influence on his entire life:

> *"I had a half-sister who got killed in 1981. And I was just 12, so that was my wake-up call in life, and what it is really about, you know. . . . Gotta prevent stuff from happening to you. You know, that's what youngsters and adults have to think about. Not, 'Oh, if this happens I'm going to do this,' but preventing it from hap-*

pening to you. So, you have to be alert about your life and which way it is going."

After the tragedy, O'Shea's parents thought a lot about how they could prevent bad things from happening to their youngest son, and they decided that the best way would be to get him out of that poisonous atmosphere. When it was time for O'Shea to go into middle school, they decided to send him to a school outside of the neighborhood.

New School, Same Life

At that time, there were a lot of programs busing children from inner-city neighborhoods to other schools. The hope was that by integrating students and putting students from disadvantaged neighborhoods into better schools, kids would learn to get along, racism would be reduced, and kids from disadvantaged backgrounds would get a better education. In O'Shea's experience, however, it didn't work out that way. He described what happened in his Rap News Network chat:

> *"So, I went up there and basically they didn't want us out there. You know, a lot of kids got bussed from the inner city to the valley and the community, the faculty really didn't want us out there. Some of them could disguise that and kind of do their job, but some of them couldn't. Some of them would let you know in so many ways. You know, so, I kind of faced a little bit [of discrimination] every day."*

But from O'Shea's perspective, the discrimination and tensions at his new school were far from the biggest thing he had to worry about. He went on to state that the atmosphere at school was nothing compared to the stress he felt on the streets of his neighborhood. In the conversation, he painted a picture of himself as a stressed-out kid with too many worldly worries on his mind:

> *"As a kid, as a youngster, I didn't care [about the atmosphere at the school]. Because to me that weren't the hardest thing I was facing. The hardest thing was when the bus dropped me off at 4 o'clock and I had to walk through the neighborhood to get back to my house. You know, that was more stressful than any of that other stuff. . . . So, I was just worried too much, worried about my neighborhood. So, it was real things every day that could affect you, but when you are black, you just can't afford the luxury of letting it bother you to the point where you can't move or function or you can't succeed."*

O'Shea's parents heard about what was happening in his new school, and they didn't like it. It wasn't long before they pulled him out of that school. By the time he was ready to enter high school, he was enrolled at Los Angeles's William Howard Taft High School—a respected public school that today boasts among its graduates a long list of famous athletes, musicians, and actors. But while O'Shea's parents could switch his school, they couldn't switch his neighborhood. Soon the events on those streets would find their way into O'Shea's writing.

Cool as Ice

If O'Shea was nervous about his world, however, he certainly didn't show it. He wasn't the type of kid to let his fear or emotions show. While still young, he was already developing a tough-as-nails attitude. He was also growing a bit of an ego. Before he even hit middle school, he thought of himself as pretty cool, so cool in fact that he had no problem walking up to Clyde's girlfriends and trying his hand at a little flirtation. It didn't upset his brother at all. In fact, Clyde seemed to get a

Ice Cube was part of a program that bused kids from the inner city to schools outside their districts. The idea was to provide kids with a better education and to reduce the racism that seemed to be growing by the day. Sometimes good intentions aren't enough.

kick out of his little brother's **bravado**. One day, he decided his ultra-cool little bro deserved a nickname, and he started calling him "Ice Cube."

Everyone started calling the slick kid Ice Cube, and no one could have guessed how popular that name would one day become. But that famous **persona** was still just in its infancy. For now, Ice Cube was just the confident, flirtatious neighborhood sports star. But when O'Shea hit high school, he took a huge leap toward becoming Ice Cube the rapper.

No matter how much they tried, Ice Cube's parents couldn't protect him from all the violence in his neighborhood. Kids his age were often involved with violence—and serious brushes with the law. Rather than take part in gang activity and other criminal ventures, Ice Cube used them in his lyrics.

One day when O'Shea was in ninth grade, he was sitting in typing class, bored to tears. Luckily, one of his best friends, whose nickname was "Kiddo," was in the class too. They could pass each other notes and provide each other with a little entertainment. That day, Kiddo asked O'Shea if he'd ever written a rap before. O'Shea and Kiddo were both big rap fans, but O'Shea had never tried to actually write a rap himself. Kiddo thought they should try, and suggested they each write one and see which one came out the best. O'Shea, who had never even considered writing a rap before that typing class, but who was already competitive by nature, agreed to the challenge and won the bet. He was just fourteen years old, and his rap career had just begun.

Years later, in an interview with Terry Gross of NPR's *Fresh Air*, Terry asked Ice Cube how his mother felt about his turning to rap music. At that time, a lot of parents didn't like this new form of music and the hip-hop culture it was part of. But Ice Cube explained that his mother didn't feel that way at all: "She didn't care what I was rapping about as long as I had a mic in my hand and not a gun."

After writing rap songs as a fourteen-year-old, Ice Cube eventually became an artist himself. Before long, he had made a name for himself as one of the pioneers of gangsta rap.

Straight Outta Compton

Ice Cube was just fourteen when he wrote his first rap song, and in just a few years, writing raps would sky-rocket him to local, then national, then international fame. But for now, he was still far from the stage and the spotlight. His rap career was in its humble beginnings, rhyming in a friend's smelly garage.

Getting in the Game

After writing that first rap song with Kiddo, Ice Cube started writing raps all the time. He soon bonded with another kid, Tony Wheatob, over the obsession. Tony's friends called him Sir Jinx. He also loved rap music, and he had some recording equipment in his garage. It wasn't the most pleasant place to hang out (Sir Jinx's dog apparently lived in the garage and wasn't exactly house-broken), but it was all they had. Sir Jinx, Ice Cube, and another friend, K-Dee, formed their first rap crew, C.I.A. (Cru' in Action) and began making tapes in their stinky makeshift studio.

Sir Jinx's digs and equipment left something to be desired, but his contacts were much more impressive. In fact, he had a cousin who was becoming a pretty famous DJ in the Los Angeles area. His name was Dr. Dre, and he was part of a group called WCWC (World Class Wreckin' Crew) their music was even on the local hip-hop station. It wasn't long before Ice Cube had the chance to rap for the up-and-coming DJ. Dr. Dre liked what he saw in the young boys—Ice Cube especially seemed to have talent with lyrics—and invited Ice Cube to hang with him and come to some of his parties. Then he invited Ice Cube and Sir Jinx to perform at his club. They wrote some rap *parodies* of songs that were popular on the radio. It was their first taste of being real rappers, out in front of a crowd. They loved it, and they knew they wanted more.

Soon after, parodying famous songs became C.I.A.'s trademark. The group made a name for itself in the local neighborhoods by rewriting and remixing current hits with profanity and heavy beats. They sold tapes of their new creations out of the back of a car. It was clever and fun, and it earned the group a local fan base. From there they began making up songs about the things they saw going down in the neighborhood. It was the start of the reality-based rap that would define Ice Cube's career. Before long, C.I.A. made its first and only album. It was a short work produced by Dr. Dre, called *My Posse*. It was completed in 1986 and released in 1987. Ice Cube was just seventeen years old.

Opportunity Knocks

Then Dr. Dre came to Ice Cube with a big opportunity. He had a friend, Eric Wright, better known as Eazy-E, who was getting into the rap business. Eazy-E had been a drug dealer, living a hardcore, dangerous life. He'd made a lot of money, but he knew time was running out. He figured there were only two ways a guy like him could end up—in prison or in a casket—and he was hoping for something a little better. He decided to take his money, get on the right side of the law before it was too late, and start a legitimate business. That's how Ruthless Records began.

So Eazy-E was starting the Ruthless Records label, but he needed some acts. That's where Dr. Dre came in. Dre was supposed to find new talent for the label and help produce their work. He had his eye on an East Coast crew called HBO (which stood for Homeboys Only) for the first record. They had a good image and delivery, but they weren't the best

If you wanted to be a hip-hop star in California, having Dr. Dre in your corner could do a lot to send you on your way. Not only was he a star, he was a producer with many contacts in the business. Dr. Dre liked to help up-and-coming artists, including Ice Cube.

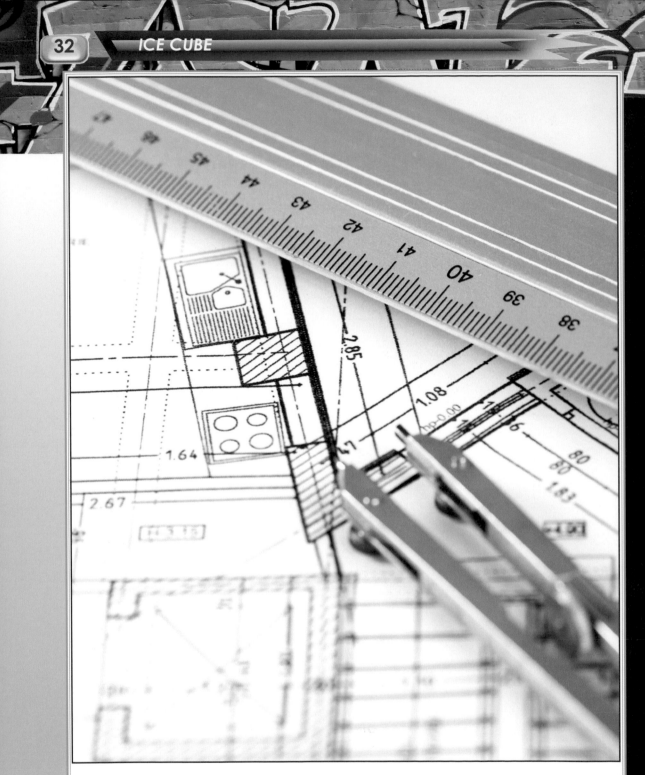

Before Ice Cube could concentrate on a music career, he had to graduate from high school. After high school, he went on to college and studied architectural drafting.

songwriters; they'd need someone to write their material. For that job, Dr. Dre had his eye on Ice Cube.

At the time, Ice Cube was holding down his first "real" job, a stint as a garage parking attendant that meant he had to get up at 4:30 a.m. and wear a highly embarrassing polyester suit. Ice Cube was more than enthusiastic about the chance to write lyrics for Eazy's new label. If nothing else, it should help restore some of his street cred . . . something that had taken a bit of a hit since he started wearing his less-than-hip parking attendant threads.

Ice Cube set to work, putting all of his energy into the lyrics of the new song that would be called "Boyz-n-the-Hood." The lyrics were raw and startling. They were about guns, gangs, drinking, even roughing up a girlfriend for getting out of line. Dre and Eazy loved it. No one had heard anything like it before. HBO had certainly never heard the likes of it before, and they refused to rap it. Disgusted, they went back east, and Dre and Eazy thought about what to do next.

Then Dr. Dre had a brilliant idea. What did they need HBO for? He, Eazy, and Ice Cube could just make the record themselves. Of course, there was the little problem of Eazy not being an MC. In fact, Eazy had never rapped before at all. But they went ahead anyway, recorded the single, got 10,000 vinyl records cut, and started selling them out of the trunk of a car. It became a big local success, and Ice Cube, Eazy, and Dre started working on two more singles: "8-Ball" and "Dopeman." Soon they were leaving their other gigs behind. Dr. Dre stepped away from WCWC while Ice Cube left C.I.A. to form a new crew: N.W.A, "Niggaz with Attitude." The three singles, "Boyz-n-the-Hood," "8-Ball," and "Dopeman" would soon reappear on a **compilation** album called *N.W.A and the Posse*, which also featured songs by other local rappers and DJs.

Detour on the Road

Ice Cube's hard-hitting lyrics were getting attention, including the attention of a well-known manager named Jerry Heller, who cut a deal to manage N.W.A But Ice Cube wasn't ready for the big time quite yet. He was just graduating from high school. He was dreaming of a music career, but the local success of their first singles didn't convince him that he'd make it in the music world. After all, rap was only just gaining its first widespread popularity, and who knew how long that popularity would last? Maybe it would keep getting bigger. Or maybe it would all be over tomorrow, and rap would land back in the dust of the ghetto where it started.

When Ice Cube's parents told him he should have a trade to fall back on if the music thing didn't work out, he listened. He decided to go to college and enrolled in the architectural drafting program at the Phoenix Institute of Technology in Arizona. Dre and Eazy couldn't believe it. Here N.W.A was on the verge of something big—they could feel it—and now their lead lyricist was going off to school. But what could they do? Ice Cube said he'd keep writing for them in his spare time, and they said his spot in the group would be waiting for him.

Over the course of the next year, Ice Cube earned a diploma in architectural drafting and design. But while he was preparing for a desk job, Eazy-E was putting out his first solo album, *Eazy-Duz-It*. He asked Ice Cube to help him with the lyrics, and juggling his studies and lyricist duties, Ice Cube wrote some raps for the album. The album came out in early 1988, caught a lot of attention, and helped set the stage for what N.W.A would do next. The group had expanded—now it also included DJ Yella and MC Ren—and was working on its first full-length album. Ice Cube decided he was done with school and got back on board with N.W.A in time for the album's release.

Catching the FBI's Eye

In 1988, N.W.A's first album, *Straight Outta Compton*, came out and turned the music world upside down. It was too hot to handle: the explicit lyrics and violent themes got it immediately banned from the airwaves. Nevertheless, the album went **platinum**, then double platinum, and became the album that defined a whole new style of music: gangsta rap.

Suddenly N.W.A was big . . . really big. And they were getting a lot of attention. Their fans loved the hardcore lyrics—raps about gang violence, street life, guns, drugs, and other harsh realities. They also loved N.W.A for their political anger and the blows they laid on authority figures, particularly the Los Angeles Police Department. The most controversial song on the album was called "F— tha Police" (censorship added), and it took dead aim at the LAPD, long known for aggressive tactics and repeatedly accused of rampant police brutality. At one point in the song, Ice Cube raps about going on a cop-killing warpath:

> *"when I'm finished, it's gonna be a bloodbath*
> *Of cops, dyin in L.A."*

That got people's attention. While some fans loved the boldness and violence of it all, critics also had a lot to say, and not all of it was good. The group's lyrics went way beyond simple profanity to something completely new: outright glorification and glamorization of gang life, law breaking, and disrespect for authority. The song's title became an inner-city slogan, and it showed up scrawled on walls, buses, and other public spaces around the country. The song got N.W.A labeled "the world's most dangerous group" and even caught the attention of the FBI. The FBI sent a letter to N.W.A's record label expressing their displeasure with the song. There could be no doubt at all: Ice Cube and N.W.A were now a force to be reckoned with.

There's something about music and movies: actors want to sing and singers want to act. But few musicians have had as successful a film career as Ice Cube.

From Hood to Hollywood

N.W.A brought Ice Cube his first widespread success and got his name out into the world, but he didn't stay with the group for long. In 1989, soon after *Straight Outta Compton* was released, he moved to New York City to start a solo career. The very next year, his first solo album, *AmeriKKKa's Most Wanted*, skyrocketed up the charts. No one had expected such a reception. After all, Ice Cube had only been known as part of N.W.A, not as a solo artist. That didn't slow his album down at all. It broke the top twenty on the *Billboard* 200 album chart and sold more than 500,000 copies in just ten days. Two months later, it was certified platinum.

The New Ice Cube

In some ways, *AmeriKKKa's Most Wanted* was more of the same: more profanity, more anger, more gangs, guns, drugs, and violence. But those who explored the album more deeply found a lot to compliment. Ice Cube was proving he had a poet's sense about lyrics, and his commentary went far deeper than the typical boasting and bravado of many gangsta rappers. His album might have been gangsta rap, but it was also political, conscious hip-hop that made a lot of intelligent insights about poverty and racism.

While critics still argued the album was sexist and demeaning toward women, one song, "It's a Man's World," was a

Ice Cube got his big break in film in 1991 with *Boyz n the Hood*. Before long, he seemed to be spending more time on the big screen than in the recording studio. The boy from the 'hood was now from Hollywood.

back-and-forth battle of the sexes between Ice Cube and powerful female rapper Yo Yo in which both rappers come out fairly equal in the end. It was not a rousing tribute to the opposite sex, but it was a far cry from many of the songs he had performed with N.W.A Even with the toned-down attitudes toward women, however, the album still had plenty of controversial themes, including songs that dissed black people who, according to the album, tried to be white.

Despite the criticism, *AmeriKKKa's Most Wanted* was a huge success and has gone down in history as one of the most important hip-hop albums of all time. More success followed. Soon after releasing his first solo album, Ice Cube put out an EP (extended play disc) called *Kill at Will* that also went platinum. Ice Cube was certainly not softening from his success. The EP's cover featured a picture of Ice Cube offering a gun (the implication being an offer to use it to "kill at will"). Inside, the music and lyrics were as hardcore as ever. But the social and political commentary was also strong, especially in the song "Dead Homiez," which explored the emotions and tragedy that families experience because of gang violence.

In 1990, family became a focus for Ice Cube for another reason. That's the year his first child was born. Ice Cube named his son O'Shea Jackson Jr., and having a child began to change his perspective of the world.

Storming Hollywood

Ice Cube was just a few years out of high school. He was a new father, and his career was going supernova. He was a famous rapper, and he was about to become a famous actor. A young director named John Singleton had written a film based on life in the gang-infested streets of South Central Los Angeles. Like the N.W.A song, he called the film *Boyz n the Hood*, and he wanted Ice Cube to play a starring role.

Ice Cube jumped at the chance, and in 1991, the film was released with Ice Cube playing alongside the likes of Cuba

with "sharp insights and unflinching looks at contemporary urban lifestyles . . . in short, it's hardcore without any gangsta **posturing**." But if the gangsta posturing was gone, the controversial topics were not. While the album talked about topics like minimum wage, teen pregnancy, and sexually transmitted diseases, it also had lyrics that seemed sexist, **homophobic**, and racist. The song "Black Korea" in particular came under fire for racist sentiments.

As most rappers do, Ice Cube answered all of his critics by saying he was just putting reality into words. He claimed that his lyrics were the truth—the words might be harsh, but the ghetto is a harsh place. Later in his career, he would soften his stance, saying that the lyrics he wrote and songs he produced were the way he saw the world through his angry, young eyes, but that he sees some things differently now. At the moment, however, there would be no softening of Ice Cubes cold, vicious words.

His next album, *The Predator*, released in 1992, was proof that the hardcore rapper wouldn't be tamed by criticism. It became the first album to ever debut at #1 on both the popular *Billboard* 200 album chart and Top R&B/Hip Hop Albums chart. It became Ice Cube's best-selling album, eventually going triple platinum. In 1992, Ice Cube also starred in his second movie, *Trespass*, and further committed to family life by marrying Kimberly Jackson. He and Kimberly would go on to have three more children.

Switching Gears

As the 1990s went on, it became clear that Ice Cube's movie career was ramping up, but his musical output was winding down. In 1993, he released *Lethal Injection*. This newest solo album seemed to be a step away from the political weight of his previous solo work, and a leap back to the gangsta rap of his N.W.A days. It sold well, hit #5 on the *Billboard* 200 and #1 on the Top R&B/Hip Hop Album chart, but it wasn't as popular with Ice Cube's fan base as his other albums had been.

After *Lethal Injection*, Ice Cube virtually disappeared from the music charts. He produced other artists' work, but there wouldn't be another Ice Cube solo album for years. But if his star was fading for a time in the music world, it was burning bright in Hollywood. In the six years between the beginning of 1993 and the end of 1998, he would appear or star in eight feature films. In 1995, Ice Cube was nominated for an

If people thought film would completely take Ice Cube out of the music scene, they were wrong. He continued to record, and he moved into producing other musicians' recordings.

NAACP Image Award—given to honor people of color for outstanding accomplishments in the arts and media—for his role in the drama *Higher Learning*.

That same year, Ice Cube's most famous film, *Friday*, came out. The comedy, also starring Chris Tucker, is a day-in-the-life of two best friends in a South Central Los Angeles neighborhood like the one Ice Cube grew up in. The movie was hugely popular with black audiences, became an instant **cult** classic,

Friday combined the talents of Ice Cube and comedian Chris Tucker as two friends in South Central Los Angeles. The movie became a huge cult classic and led to two sequels.

and spawned the sequels *Next Friday* (2000) and *Friday After Next* (2002).

Back to the Music

In 1998, Ice Cube went back to music to release his first solo album in five years. The album, *War & Peace Volume I (The War Disc)*, was the first of a two-part project. The second part, *The Peace Disc*, was released in 2000. The albums never did get far with fans, and there would be another six-year hiatus before Ice Cube released another solo album.

In 1998, however, Ice Cube's skills expanded into other areas. He had his debut as a feature-film writer and director with *The Players Club*, in which he also acted. In 1999, he played perhaps his most challenging role to that date when he starred in *Three Kings* alongside George Clooney, Mark Wahlberg, and Hollywood newcomer Spike Jonze. The film, which is about four American soldiers scheming to steal gold from Saddam Hussein's bunkers, is set during the 1991 Iraqi uprising that took place after the first Gulf War.

In 2002, Ice Cube had his biggest film success since *Friday*, and perhaps the biggest success of his entire film career. It came in a comedy called *Barbershop*. In it, Ice Cube was finally able to play a character completely unlike the thugs, gangstas, action figures, and other tough-guy roles he so commonly played. This time he was a young man who was expecting a baby and unhappily managing the family barbershop. Ice Cube, who was by now a well-established father and family man, could relate a lot to the film and enjoyed the opportunity to let other aspects of himself show in his work. The sequel, *Barbershop 2: Back in Business* followed in 2004. Ice Cube had made his mark on the music world. Now his mark in Hollywood was permanent and undeniable as well.

Ice Cube's film career has only picked up speed with the new millennium. In 2007, he starred in *Are We Done Yet?* In this photo, he and some of his costars pose at the premiere, held at the Apollo Theater.

5

Rage for Change

In 2005, some people began to wonder what had become of Ice Cube. That's because the one-time gangsta rapper shocked many of his fans that year by taking on a completely new film role: the lead actor in a family comedy called *Are We There Yet?* It was a lightweight story of a bachelor, Nick (played by Ice Cube), who falls for Suzanne, a mother of two. He likes Suzanne, but isn't crazy about the kids . . . and they can't stand him. But realizing he can't win over Suzanne if he doesn't win over the kids, he embarks on a plan to get the kids on his side. What results is a series of comic misadventures that conclude in a predictably happy ending of love and family bliss.

Where Has the Bad Boy Gone?

When the PG feature came out (to good sales but terrible reviews), some people wondered what had happened to their sneering, venomous rapper. Could this family-friendly comic character be the same man? And could the tough-guy image his rap career was built on survive after softening up for the kids? In an interview with morphizm.com, Ice Cube said that to be committed to his acting career he couldn't worry about maintaining that tough-as-nails persona all the time. He explained that, at the end of the day, he didn't just want to be gangsta rapper. He wanted to have a multifaceted career that had something for everyone to enjoy:

> *"I've been around so long it seems like, that it would be kind of crazy to plan my career around an image. For acting, in films, it's all about giving up of yourself, emotionally, being in the moment. . . . With records, you can be one kind of way, and records show one slice of my personality I've chosen to make public. But with movies you have to open up. I don't want to be delegated to just doing hood movies, you know, trying to keep it real, so to speak. I've been in the game a long time, and my place in hip-hop history hopefully is in stone somewhere, with NWA, and it's all about growing and expanding my audience. The* Friday *movies were R-rated,* Barbershop *PG-13. And here,* Are We There Yet? *is a PG movie. Kids love those other movies, but they're not geared for them. But I'm not trying to be Eddie Murphy and just kind of do kids' movies, and be a wholesome actor. I want to do a range of things, and this is just part of it."*

At the end of the day, it seems simply that the young gangsta rapper is growing up. In his chat for Rap News Network, he talked about how much his perspective has changed over the course of his career. He said he's no longer the young, angry kid yelling obscenities and rapping about dope and guns. Now he says he has a different perspective, and he'd rather try to change the world than just rant and complain about it:

> *"The music that I did when I was young, yeah, I wholeheartedly stand by it, that's what I was feeling, that's what I said, that's what was recorded. . . . As you get older, you start to realize, if you want to make an impact on people, you can't just yell 'the world sucks' from the highest mountaintop. I have to do things, I have to do things that really affect people. . . . At some point you got to actually do things that affect what you are talking about to try to change it. And my thing was, before I got into Hollywood, it looked a lot different than it do now. And I believe that I have had something to do with changing that."*

Still Tough

Fans, however, need not worry that their beloved tough guy is gone for good. He reappeared in Ice Cube's next film, the 2005 action feature *XXX: State of the Union*. In 2006, he was back in music too. His eighth solo studio album, *Laugh Now, Cry Later,* was as hard-hitting as ever. It was also the most brutally critical in its politics, with its criticisms of President George W. Bush and the Iraq war. It could be called Ice Cube's comeback album, as it debuted at #4 on the *Billboard* 200 and #2 on the Top R&B/Hip Hop Albums chart. A year after its release, it was still selling well, and had already gone platinum.

In 2006, Ice Cube also played a huge role in a hard-hitting television series. This time, however, that role was behind the cameras. He was one of the creators behind the six-part FX series, *Black. White.*—a reality series in which two families, one black and one white, traded races. Each family donned makeup to allow them to pass as the other race and tried to see the world through the other family's eyes. The show tried to be educational and transformative, but it got a lot of criticism, many critics saying it fell short of its goals and actually reinforced some **stereotypes**.

As of now, it seems that Ice Cube may be returning to a focus on the music. Two more solo albums are reportedly in the works. *Raw Footage* is expected to debut in 2007, and *Growin' Up in tha Hood* is planned for a 2008 release date. But movies are still big on the agenda, with the sequel, *Are We Done Yet?*, hitting theaters in 2007, and two other films, *The Extractors* and *First Sunday*, planned for 2008.

Not Everything Has Changed

Over the years, a lot has changed for Ice Cube. Today he is one of the most important (not to mention wealthiest) hip-hop artists in history and a powerful force in Hollywood. He's come a long way from his South Central roots. But in his chat for Rap News Network, Ice Cube revealed that some things haven't changed much from what he witnessed in his early days. He said that, though a lot of progress has been made, one thing is still a major obstacle for him and for all minority people in America: racism. He said that racism is still the number-one challenge to minorities in the film industry as well:

> *"You know, the same old thing, racism. . . . That's to me the biggest obstacle. . . . It's just trying to get past the same old hurdles that this country has always faced in this business. The same old problems, you got to get through them. Some people can see through that,*

some people can't, but you just got to keep on convincing people that you can do it."

While he clearly takes issue with the racism that is still prevalent today, he also seemed to have concerns about other aspects of his profession. In the interview, he went on to tell the young people he was chatting with that while rap music is all about boasting and bragging, and so much of what is on

When *Are We Done Yet?* was released, more and more people wondered if Ice Cube had left the music business. He had appeared in a string of successful films, and it seemed as though there was no stopping this new movie icon.

television is bling and materialism, the most important things are the things you can't buy:

> *"People have to look at their body as the best thing that they will ever own. You never own nothing better than your body. I mean all these trinkets—I have six cars, but I can only drive one at a time. You know, you got this nice car, but you can't see yourself in it. Only other people can see you driving down the*

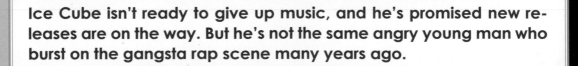

Ice Cube isn't ready to give up music, and he's promised new releases are on the way. But he's not the same angry young man who burst on the gangsta rap scene many years ago.

street. At some point it becomes like it don't matter. It always matters when you don't have it and you want it, and when you get it, you really realize it don't matter . . . no matter how rich you are, if your body is not healthy, then you are not going to enjoy that money anyway, and they're not going to put it in the casket with you when they puts you in the ground. So health is the most important thing in life."

At the end of the day, after all the success, the controversy, the albums, and the films, it seems Ice Cube has come full circle. As a kid, his family was always the most important thing. He says his father always told him to focus on family first, saying, "those famous people don't put no food on your table." Now, being famous is what puts food on Ice Cube's table, but it's all for his wife, daughter, and three sons.

Some people might wonder how being a hardcore, gangsta rapper can happily coexist with being a father. Some might ask what type of role model Ice Cube can be for his kids and whether his children will respect him as a father and authority figure when they hear the things he says as a rapper. But all evidence seems to show that Ice Cube's rapper and father roles are getting along just fine.

In his interview with Terry Gross for NPR's *Fresh Air*, Ice Cube said that he raises his kids to have self-respect and to understand the proper **context** of all the things they see in the media, whether it be in music, movies, magazines, or even on the news. He went on to say that he believes the best way to raise kids is to show them decency and respect. He says it's the best way to treat any person, and that if all people treated each other with respect, there would be a lot less violence in the world, and (he could add) gangsta rappers would have a lot less to rage about.

June 15,

1969   O'Shea Jackson—Ice Cube—is born.

1970s   Hip-hop begins in New York City.

1981   Ice Cube's half-sister is killed, and it is a wake-up call for him.

1986   N.W.A forms.

1987   C.I.A.'s *My Posse* is released.

1988   *Eazy-Duz-It* is released, for which Ice Cube wrote many of the lyrics.

1988   *Straight Outta Compton* by N.W.A is released.

1989   Ice Cube moves to New York to begin a solo career.

1990   *AmeriKKKa's Most Wanted* is released.

1990   Ice Cube becomes a father for the first time.

1991   Ice Cube costars in his first film, *Boyz n the Hood*.

1992   *The Predator* becomes the first album to debut at #1 on the popular *Billboard* 200 album chart and Top R&B/Hip Hop Albums chart.

1992   Ice Cube gets married.

1995   Ice Cube is nominated for an NAACP Image Award for his performance in *Higher Learning*.

1998   Ice Cube debuts as a feature-film writer and director with *The Players Club*.

1999 Ice Cube costars with George Clooney and Mark Wahlberg in *Three Kings*.

2000 Ice Cube is honored with a Lifetime Achievement Award at the Hip-Hop Music Awards.

2002 Ice Cube stars in the hit film *Barbershop*.

2005 Ice Cube receives a Lifetime Achievement Award at the Soul Train Music Awards.

2006 *Laugh Now, Cry Later*, Ice Cube's first album in six years, is released and goes platinum.

2006 Ice Cube is the co-creator of *Black. White*, an FX reality series.

2006 Ice Cube is one of the honorees at the VH1 Hip Hop Honors.

2007 *Raw Footage* is released.

Albums

1990   *AmeriKKKa's Most Wanted*

1990   *Kill at Will* (EP)

1991   *Death Certificate*

1992   *The Predator*

1993   *Lethal Injection*

1998   *War & Peace—Volume 1 (The War Disc)*

2000   *War & Peace—Volume 2 (The Peace Disc)*

2006   *Laugh Now, Cry Later*

2007   *Raw Footage*

2008   *Growin' Up in tha Hood*

Number-One Singles

1990   "AmeriKKKa's Most Wanted"

1992   "Wicked"

1993   "It Was a Good Day"

1993   "Check Yo Self" (with Das EFX)

1996   "Bow Down" (with Westside Connection)

1998   "Pushin' Weight" (with Short Khop)

DVDs

2003   *Making of a Don*

2003   *Ice Cube: The Videos*

2006   *Ice Cube on DVD*

Films

1991   *Boyz n the Hood*

1992   *Trespass*

1994   *The Glass Shield*

1995   *Higher Learning*

1995   *Friday*

1997   *Dangerous Ground*

1997   *Anaconda*

1998   *The Players Club*

1998   *I Got the Hook Up*

1999   *Three Kings*

1999   *Thicker Than Water*

2000   *Next Friday*

2001   *Ghosts of Mars*

2002   *All About the Benjamins*

2002	*Barbershop*
2002	*Friday After Next*
2004	*Torque*
2004	*Barbershop 2: Back in Business*
2005	*Are We There Yet?*
2005	*XXX: State of the Union*
2007	*Are We Done Yet?*
2008	*The Extractors*
2008	*First Sunday*

Awards/Recognition

2000 Blockbuster Entertainment Award: Favorite Action Team (for Three Kings); Hip-Hop Music Awards: Lifetime Achievement Award.

2002 MECCA Movie Award: Acting Award.

2005 Soul Train Music Award: Lifetime Achievement Award.

2006 VH1 Hip-Hop Honors: 2006 Honoree.

Books

Chang, Jeff. *Can't Stop Won't Stop: A History of the Hip-Hop Generation*. New York: Picador, 2005.

Kusek, Dave, and Gerd Leonhard. *The Future of Music: Manifesto for the Digital Music Revolution*. Boston, Mass.: Berkley Press, 2005.

Light, Alan (ed.). *The Vibe History of Hip Hop*. New York: Three Rivers Press, 1999.

McIver, Joel. *Ice Cube: Attitude*. London: Sanctuary Publishing, 2002.

Orr, Tamara. *Ice Cube*. Hockessin, Del.: Mitchell Lane, 2006.

Web Sites

Ice Cube
www.icecube.com

Ice Cube Official Web Site
www.icecubemusic.com

Ice Cube on My Space
www.myspace.com/icecube

Glossary

bravado—A real or pretend show of courage or boldness.

cinematic—Relating to movies.

compilation—Something created by bringing things together from different sources.

context—The circumstances or events in which something exists or takes place.

cult—Having to do with extreme or excessive admiration for a person, activity, form of music, book, or movie.

genre—A category into which an artistic work can be placed based on subject, form, or style.

homophobic—Showing an irrational hatred, disapproval, or fear of homosexuality and its culture.

icon—A symbol or emblem of a particular culture or way of life.

mainstream—The ideas, actions, and values that are most widely accepted by a group or society.

parodies—Writings or music that deliberately copy another work in a funny or ridiculing way.

persona—The personality that someone shows the outside world.

platinum—A designation that a recording has sold a million copies.

posturing—Exhibiting an artificial attitude.

sampling—Taking a short musical phrase from one recording and using it in another.

segregationist—Someone who practices or believes in segregation, the purposeful separation of individuals, primarily based on race.

sexism—The tendency to treat people of cultural stereotypes of their sex.

stereotypes—Oversimplified images or ideas, often based on inaccurate and incomplete information, that one person or group holds about another.

venomous—Full of malice, spite, or extreme hostility.

Index

About the Author

Toby G. Hamilton was born in 1979 in Binghamton, NY. As an author and illustrator, Toby is interested in art's power as a tool of self-expression, social commentary, and political activism. Toby is especially interested in hip-hop's role in twenty-first century America and its increasing power as a revolutionary force around the world.

Picture Credits

Gabber, David / PR Photos: p. 51
Harris, Glenn / PR Photos: front cover, pp. 2, 18, 35, 44
Hernandez, Noah / PR Photos: p. 43
iStockphoto: pp. 25, 38
   Bergman, Hal: p. 16
   Lugo, Jason: p. 26
   Manciu, Andreea: p. 32
   Stein, Daniel: p. 11
   Viisimaa, Peeter: p. 41
Moore, Anthony G. / PR Photos: p. 46
PR Photos: pp. 8, 28, 52
Thompson, Terry / PR Photos: p. 31

To the best knowledge of the publisher, all other images are in the public domain. If any image has been inadvertently uncredited, please notify Harding House Publishing Service, Vestal, New York 13850, so that rectification can be made for future printings.